Staying Sane as You Homeschool

Balancing Your Priorities

Kathy Kuhl

D1316168

To my husband

Learn Differently LLC
P.O. Box 711241
Herndon, Virginia 20171-1241

www.LearnDifferently.com

Printed in the United States of America.

Scripture quotations are from The Holy Bible, English Standard Edition ®
© 2001 by Crossway Bibles, a publishing ministry of Good News Publishers.
Used by permission. All rights reserved.

Unless full names are given, names of parents and children are changed to preserve their privacy.

Book design and cover design by Martha Leone.

Introduction

I am not a parenting expert. I am a mother and a veteran homeschooler who has gone through her share of frustrating days, worries, and guilt. But I have learned from many wise people, and I love to share what has helped me. As my first book pulled together the resources I wish I had when I started to homeschool a child with learning challenges, here I bring together insights from many sources to help you contemplate your priorities and find your balance as you homeschool.

Please think of this book as "one beggar telling another where to find bread," as D.T. Niles wrote. I invite you to make notes as you write, underline, and especially, to stop and take time to think how these ideas can help you and your family to stay sane.

Chapter 1
No one said it would be easy

Homeschooling can be wonderful for families, for education, and for instilling values. But no one promised it would be easy.

Many worthwhile tasks can be difficult. Raising children, for example, is the most rewarding work I have ever undertaken. But I would never call it easy, even though I happen to have had the cutest children on the planet, who are now fascinating, kind adults.

Let's first discuss why you are reading this book. What is making homeschooling a struggle for you now? Consider a few scenarios:

- Are you a new homeschooler, feeling daunted by the responsibility? The other homeschoolers you know may seem confident and prepared. Perhaps you recently attended your first homeschool convention, and are overwhelmed with information and insights. Maybe you are sitting at home, pouring over curriculum and catalogs, wondering, "Am I going to ruin this child's education? Am I going to wreck my children?"

- Are you doing too much? In the back of your mind, you know something has to go, but you can't bear to drop anything. How do you choose?

- Are you struggling to find the right methods, curriculum, or pace for one or more of your children? Do you have a child who is gifted, discouraged, struggling—or perhaps all three at once? You may not be able to tell if the child has a legitimate learning problem or is just being lazy.

- Are you too tired? Have you lost your enthusiasm, your joy, or your vision for your homeschool? Some of you are going through the motions, weary, and maybe a little bitter.

- Is your child angry and resisting homeschooling?

- Maybe the source of stress is obvious—a new baby, a new home, a spouse deployed, a chronic illness, a divorce, or a death. Sometimes it is reasonable to feel stressed.

No matter why you are feeling stressed or overwhelmed, there are solutions. Certain principles can help you in all these situations. In this book, we will look at our attitudes and assumptions first, because they can make homeschooling harder without our knowing it. Then we will consider steps we can take to keep going and to take care of our families and ourselves.

Let's get started.

Personally, I don't like to think that I might be part of my problems. But sometimes I am. It is no fun to look over my life to find where I am making things harder, but not looking is worse. As Jeremiah wrote, "The heart is deceitful above all things," (Jeremiah 17:9), which means, among other things, that we are good at conning ourselves.

That is why we need to make time to think. Pondering is not popular in modern Western culture. We spend time and money providing ourselves with pleasant distractions that keep us from thinking too much. When we do think, it tends to be unproductive worry, round and round, rather than productive analysis.

Our habits can conspire against becoming thoughtful about what we do. When I drive away from my home, the habit of turning on the car radio can keep me from reflecting on the conversation I just had, or the needs of people I am going to see. It takes regular effort to make time to think.

As you continue reading, consider what attitudes you may have slipped into, and what assumptions you could be making that could be crippling your homeschool.

Chapter 2
Back to school?

Do schools know best? Should we do it their way? Some of us even wonder if our children might be better off in school. We don't like to say it out loud. What would our friends think?

Every family needs to choose how to educate their children. I know families committed to homeschooling who have put children in school because of difficult circumstances. I think homeschooling is great, but is not my place to second-guess your choices. You are responsible for choosing what is best for your child and your family. I want to help you consider the options wisely. If you are discouraged about your home-school, it is easy to idealize the alternatives. I have.

Leave it to the pros

The first way we can idealize schools is to think that professional educators must teach better than we do. Especially if we are struggling, it is easy to assume that a teacher would do a better job.

But even if you live near a great school, with wonderful teachers—and not all of us do—it won't be trouble-free. As deeply as the teachers may care for your child's success, as experienced as they may be, they have limited options and resources. They have many other children to help. In January, they may not be able to change curriculum, as home-schoolers can. They cannot let the wiggly girl chew gum to help her focus, or put the distractible boy to work in a quiet room by himself. They cannot let the child do math under the dining room table, as I did one year. They can't build a unit around your child's special interest.

Teachers have lots to do: prepare students for standardized tests, attend meetings, complete paperwork, prepare lessons, grade papers—and teach! Society keeps thinking of more for the schools to do, leaving less time for reading aloud and for the arts. Though every teacher I know puts in extra hours, they cannot give your child much time one-on-one. And being in a special class is no panacea. A homeschooler who had been a special education teacher thought that teaching was tougher in school than at home. "In a special education classroom," she wrote, "there may be up to twelve students with different strengths and weaknesses. What works for two might not work for all twelve."

When children are shy or slow to pick up social cues, their parents may think that spending the day with many people will lead to more friendships and improved social skills. It might for some children. But crowds can be lonely places. Several families I interviewed said that having to work on social skills and academic skills simultaneously made school much harder.

Feeling burned out? Putting your child in school won't free you of responsibility for your child's education. You will spend hours communicating with the school. (One kindergarten teacher told parents, "If you believe half of what you hear about the school, I'll believe half of what I hear about your home.") And if your child has special needs, it's even harder. You will attend meetings and learn laws, acronyms, and policies. You may struggle to get your child the help he or she needs. (Some parents told me they homeschool to avoid the stress of dealing with school.) And after school, you'll tutor your child when you both are tired. Don't think enrolling a child in school will make everything easy.

Let's have school at home
A second way we idealize schools is to let them be the standard for our homeschools. Anxious new homeschoolers may buy school desks or ring a bell at the start of the day. While a child-size chair and a writing surface at the right height for your child are great ideas, you can homeschool anywhere and any way that suits you and your child.

It is easy to forget the freedom we have when we homeschool. We may adopt methods our teachers used. The danger is in adopting approaches without thinking about whether they serve our children and us well. Schools have lectures, bells, and textbooks because that is the most efficient way to teach a large group of students, not because it is the best way to teach every child. As one mother of a struggling learner told me, "When you are trying to duplicate the school environment in a home, keep in mind that it didn't work in school; that's why he's at home."

Veteran homeschoolers can slip back into the "school mentality" as the years go by. If your homeschool is in a rut, have you been unconsciously assuming that the ways you were taught are the ways to teach? There are new methods and resources to explore.

Chapter 3
We've always done it that way

The world is changing, so our children not only need to learn, they must learn new ways to learn, so that they can work and serve their communities in the years ahead. Our homeschooling needs to be open to change, too.

New tools

One way our homeschools can change is by using new tools. Visit a homeschool convention and walk through the vendor hall. Every year I find tools I never imagined. This year I saw ways to program robotic toy bugs, a new way to teach typing, cleverly designed software, and other creative ways to teach.

If you have a child with learning challenges, take time to keep up with new developments in assistive technology. Assistive technology is any tool that helps compensate for or work around a disability. That means everything that helps— simple tools like large balls for wiggly children to sit on, weighted vests, and curiously shaped pencils that are easier to hold correctly—but especially the quickly evolving world of technological tools.

I will mention a few current favorites: the Time Timer (a visual timer), tiny digital voice recorders, WordQ word prediction software, SpeakQ dictation software, LifeScribe Pens that link written notes to audio recordings and make them searchable on a computer, and many iPad apps. But this field changes so fast no single website is keeping up, much less a book. On my website, www.learndifferently.com, I post new links and books as I find them.

People change

More important than learning about how tools are changing is being aware of how we change. If you have been homeschooling a few years, consider how you have changed your teaching style. Some parents start out with a great deal of structure—"Just tell me which curriculum to buy and how to teach it"—and become more relaxed. It wasn't until my third year of homeschooling that I was comfortable enough to create the kind of science unit I needed for a bright, distractible, dyslexic twelve-year-old.

Your children certainly will change, too. We cannot let our view of our children hold them back. My daughter's kindergarten teacher said,

"She is shy. She will always be shy. That's just how she is." Three years later, another teacher saw her differently: "Shy? No, she's not shy. She just doesn't speak up unless she has something to say."

Or take my son. When he was nine, we thought he was big enough to go on longer hikes. But unless he could throw sticks in a creek, he was bored. Three years later, he went on his first outing with the Boy Scouts. He loved it! Every summer for four years, he and his father spent a week hiking and canoeing with the Scouts, and took many other weekend hikes preparing themselves for those summer treks. If we had just said, "No, when he was nine, he hated hiking," he and his dad would have missed those wonderful experiences.

The same can be true with academic interests. Sometimes the girl who hates math becomes the young woman who finds the patterns of higher math fascinating. The boy who hates to write becomes a successful author. Be flexible in your notions of your child's strengths, weakness, and interests.

Learning styles and kinds of intelligence

We also can get stuck in a rut regarding learning styles. Many parents have read about learning styles, and know that some people prefer to learn by seeing, others by hearing, and others by doing. You may know what your children prefer.

If not, I wouldn't worry about it. Many have studied the effects of tailoring instruction to the student's learning style. Howard Pashler's review of the scientific research revealed:
- People can say how they prefer to receive information,
- People differ in that they have "specific aptitudes for different kinds of thinking and processing different kinds of information,"
- But there is "virtually no evidence" that tailoring instruction to the students' learning styles improves their performance.

So while the notion of adapting your teaching to your students' learning styles is very popular, there is no proof that it helps.

Whatever you think is the way your child learns best, whatever they prefer, a multisensory approach is a good idea. Let them hear it, see it, say it, feel it—even smell it! As Carol Barnier says in *The Big WHAT NOW Book of Learning Styles*, it is important not to let your sense of your child's strengths limit you to one approach.

It is good to know what is hard for your children, and to give them some practice in that area. But for most of their instruction, don't teach in a way that is hard for them. If a child has, say, an auditory processing disorder, look for therapies and methods to help them, but be sure to provide "work-arounds," that is, accommodations. Don't expect them to learn mainly from lecture, or to do well with oral questions, or to remember detailed assignments that you give only orally.

Thinking in terms of your child's strengths is vital to your success in homeschooling. You may find it helpful to think through Howard Gardner's theory of multiple intelligences. Gardner, like many others, found the way intelligence is defined and measured in the Stanford-Binet IQ test to be too limited. Clearly there are many ways to be intelligent. Think of all the different kinds of smart people you know: musicians who can improvise or sight-read, the golf pro who can see exactly what's wrong with your swing, the potter who can turn a lump of clay into a cup before your eyes, the store clerk who can cheer a grumpy customer.

Noticing these many different kinds of ability, Gardner developed a list of kinds of intelligence. The first two are what a standard IQ test and the Scholastic Aptitude Test try to measure, but you can see there is much more to intelligence than that.

Whether you buy Gardner's theory or not, his categories give you one way to consider your child's abilities:

- Linguistic intelligence: ability with spoken or written words, good verbal memory.
- Logical-mathematical intelligence: abstract reasoning, manipulating symbols, seeing complex patterns, scientific investigation.
- Spatial intelligence: the ability to visualize models of the spatial world in your head and to manipulate and use them. Architects, artisans, surgeons, and artists need this ability.
- Musical intelligence: heightened sensitivity to sound, meter, pitch, melody, timbre; the ability to compose. (Think of Beethoven, who kept composing even when deaf.)
- Bodily-kinesthetic intelligence: excellent control of one's body and the ability to handle objects skillfully. Athletes, dancers, jugglers, surgeons, and artisans show this intelligence.
- Interpersonal intelligence: awareness of the needs and moods of others and the ability to motivate, work with, and lead them. Leaders, teachers, and salespeople need these skills.

- Intrapersonal intelligence: introspection, knowing yourself, your strengths and weaknesses; and the ability to predict your own reactions and use that knowledge to succeed. Writers, theologians, and philosophers use these skills.
- Naturalistic: being well attuned to and able to nurture the environment around you. Farmers and naturalists show this ability.
- Existential: heightened ability to consider spiritual and metaphysical reality, beyond your senses, such as infinity. Theologians, philosophers, and physicists need this intelligence.

Intelligence can be developed. As you exercise different parts of your brain, your neurons grow more connections and you can develop new strengths. Just as with muscles, brains benefit from practice, if it is the right kind of practice. Don't be too quick to write off areas as hopeless, but do focus on strengths.

Here's a personal example: Bodily-kinesthetic intelligence is not my forte, but it is one of my mother's. She lettered in tennis in high school and continued to improve her game even into her sixties. As she tried to teach me tennis, she could have watched me chase balls for months and given up because I didn't have her natural ability. But despite my slow thinking in this area ("Where's the ball going to be in one second, two seconds?" "How long is my reach with this racquet?" "How do I aim?"), with her patience and lots of practice, she taught me to serve.

As you think about learning styles and kinds of intelligence, think about what your own strengths are. Be aware of your strengths so that you don't confuse them with what is best for your child. Just because a diagram helps you make sense of a concept does not mean it will help your child. More words often help me, but they befuddle my son. How boring it would be if we were all the same!

The bottom line is:
- Don't worry too much about learning styles.
- Pay attention to your child's strengths and weaknesses.
- Give some practice to strengthen areas of weakness.
- Build on their strengths.
- Use a multisensory approach.
- Try new approaches, since our children change.

Chapter 4
Never good enough

We all want the best for our children. Our search for those good things
can teach us about our attitudes. Is a sense of entitlement or perfectionism
spoiling our efforts? Unnoticed by us, they can frustrate us and our families.

Though homeschoolers once only had limited access to published
curriculum, now we can purchase from among hundreds of curricula,
thousands of websites, millions of books. It can be hard to figure out
which to choose. We can become grumpy when we don't see what we
want. How easily a sense of entitlement that can start creeping into our
thinking: "I don't ask much. I only want...."

Those of us with children with challenges feel the stakes are even
higher. As we search for the best therapy, treatment, or technique, are
we becoming hard to live with?

The perfect solutions we seek may not exist. I may find a pretty
good math or reading curriculum, or a helpful program for my child's
areas of struggle, but problems remain. I can keep looking, but I must
not make myself—or my family—miserable because I have not found a
perfect solution yet.

Sometimes good enough is good enough. The search for an ideal
approach can distract you from other needs because it can feel like a vir-
tuous endeavor, a hunt to save your homeschool or your child. But ask
yourself if you are using your time and energy wisely. Do you need to
make do with pretty good materials? Instead of more searching, would
it be better to spend that time taking your children on a walk, or reading them a story? Perhaps you can begin developing your own material.

High standards are good. But the urge for perfection can sour into
perfectionism. How do you know if you are turning into a perfectionist?
Do you:
- Set impossible standards?
- Become overly upset with mistakes?
- Doubt your own worth if you don't complete tasks perfectly?
- Find yourself unable to adjust your goals in a crisis or in light
  of other needs?

Perfectionism is an insistence on finding or making everything perfect—at the expense of your peace of mind or your relationships. Sometimes, just noticing this trend can help you fight that way of thinking. But at its most severe, it can be part of an anxiety disorder or an obsessive-compulsive disorder. If you have trouble combating these kinds of feelings, seek a wise counselor.

Another problem with perfectionism is that it can rub off on our children. They might have inherited a perfectionist temperament. What do my children learn if they see me overreacting when I can't find my car keys? We can count on our children to imitate just what we don't want them to!

Instead of torturing ourselves and those around us when we can't find what we want, or can't do as we want, we need to demonstrate to our children how to cope with disappointments and mistakes. Some children learn these skills by watching and growing. But others need to be carefully and repeatedly taught how to think about situations and how to deal with feelings. Some have difficulty putting feelings into words.

So we show them by talking about feelings and coping. For example, I might say one of the following:

"I'm feeling angry with myself for losing my keys again. I am worried that we won't get you to practice on time. I am going to take a couple deep breaths and pray."

"I had my keys when I got home last night. I'll retrace my steps."

"Let me brainstorm about what I can do if I cannot find the keys. Maybe Sam's mom could give you a ride."

Also, the quest for perfection can drive us crazy as we homeschool if we are expecting perfect attitudes from our family. Face it: your child may never thank you for that excellent math lesson you prepared so carefully. Be realistic. Studying is your child's job, and few of us thank the boss for the job. So if your children are unexcited about home-school, but civil about doing their schoolwork, treat them as you would like to be treated. Give them some breathing room. The book of Ecclesiastes says: "Do not take to heart all the things that people say, lest you hear your servant cursing you. Your heart knows that many times you yourself have cursed others."(Ecclesiastes 7:21-22.) Mutual respect, not mutual nitpicking, will help your homeschool flourish.

Chapter 5
Poor baby!

Are we sheltering our children or coddling them? We have a duty to protect our children and a duty to prepare them for life. Is that first duty looming so large in your mind that you are ignoring the second?

If a child is hurting, protecting them is our first instinct. Some children do need special sheltering:

- Have you pulled a child out of school because she is discouraged, hopeless, or has no desire to learn? Maybe your son is like Nancy's, who said: "I had a third grader who couldn't read, had zero self-esteem, was so full of anger, just hated everything, and cried all the time." With a child like this, you need to "de-school," that is, make your home a haven of fun, educational activities. Read to them. Start slowly with these burned-out learners and give them time to recover. Listen to what they want to learn about, and build from there.

- Other children are hurting for different reasons, such as the loss of a pet, sibling, grandparent, or parent, a parent's deployment or divorce, or a serious illness.

- Some children suffer from depression and need special help. Depression looks different in children and teens than it does in adults. Barbara Ingersoll and Sam Goldstein's book, *Lonely, Sad, and Angry: How to Help Your Unhappy Child*, explains what to look for. If you suspect your child might be depressed, talk to a pastor, licensed counselor, or psychologist.

These are times when children need special sheltering and help. But ultimately, we want to help them learn to get along without us. Though our goals for our children vary with our principles, I think all parents want to produce honest, hardworking, loving, independent adults. Somewhere Dorothy Sayers wrote, "All good children want to grow up." We see that acted out when little ones dress up like Mom or Dad or imitate them. If all good children want to grow up, then all good parents should want them to.

I sometimes do too much for my children, but I have a husband and friends who help me see it. My goal is for my children to grow up, not for me to feel needed or sentimental. Effective parenting means not coddling or isolating a child. It's about nurturing, strengthening, and equipping them for a life of useful service.

Greg Harris discussed this in "Outgrowing the Greenhouse," in *The Home School Court Report*. As young seedlings start in a greenhouse, sheltered from cold and drought, our children's lives start in our families under our constant supervision. Harris explains that plants next are moved to a cold frame for "hardening," an intermediate step with much less temperature control that prepares the young plants for life in the field. What Harris called the "cold frame" stage for teens involves letting them make decisions and moral choices, letting them see you do so, and discussing how you think about these questions.

Whether we are discussing morals, worldview, or making wise decisions (How do I schedule my schoolwork? Where should I apply for a job? Is this a good person for me to spend time with?), the "cold frame" idea is a helpful image for parents. Our long-term goal is for them to become as self-sufficient as their abilities allow. We cannot decide everything for them until they are eighteen or twenty-five, and then expect them to make wise decisions overnight. We must begin to let them make decisions and experience some of the unpleasant consequences of bad choices.

If you have a child with learning challenges, it can take longer for those lessons to sink in, even longer than the average teen. Keep reminding yourself that one of your goals is their independence. Keep teaching and demonstrating how to make wise decisions and letting them practice. It would be easier to keep deciding for them, but it will choke their independence and self-esteem.

Recently we celebrated when our youngest child, at age twenty-three, moved into his first apartment. Some friends have expressed sympathy that we are now empty nesters. We do miss him, and the house is oddly quiet, but we are happy for him that he has taken this next step toward independence. My tall son is standing a little taller now because of this move.

Chapter 6
My child's success, my success

Naturally, we want our children to succeed. We love them and wish them all good things. In areas where we have enjoyed success, we would like them to as well. But success and failure each come with different challenges to meet.

The mom or dad who enjoyed sports and appreciates how they can build body and character naturally wants the child to play sports. The straight-A students become parents who hope their children excel academically. But when our children don't succeed as we would like or don't even like what we like, we can be tempted to insist on success in particular areas because those are important to us. Those of us who don't insist may still be frustrated or annoyed with our children.

When my daughter was small, she once asked, "Daddy, do you own me?" He explained that God owned her, and that our job was to take care of her and help her grow up. Whether we believe in God or not, we ought to shudder at the thought of owning our children. Who can know what gifts will emerge from the growing young people we have the privilege of raising? Who has the wisdom to plot another person's life?

Since we don't own our children, we ought to act and think accordingly. We are caretakers, responsible to do our best to help our children grow up to be the best people they can be. We have to nurture their abilities, with a humble awareness that we make mistakes and miss things about our children's gifts, needs, and passions. Those change, too. It may take time and new circumstances to reveal them.

That caretaker view of parenting should affect how we view their failures as we teach them. Suppose your child has not mastered the times tables, despite years of effort. Or perhaps your teenager failed chemistry or driver's education, or failed to get into any of the colleges he wanted to attend. Their failures do not mean you are a failure. You may need a new approach; you may need help identifying a learning disability. Look for ways to strengthen your child's weaknesses. Look for accommodations to work around their problems, but don't despair. You may only need time and patience.

My self-worth and my success are not defined by my child's income or their outcome. We love our kids, but we are not our kids. Don't over-identify with them. Our children are responsible to do their best, be men and women of integrity, and work hard. I find that believing in a God who rules over our circumstances, and trusting him even after my best efforts fail or I don't get what I want, is a comfort and a relief. It doesn't reduce me to fatalism or give me an excuse to do nothing. To the contrary, it means I must answer to a higher authority, like any caretaker.

It also means when our children have not yet succeeded, academically, financially, or in any way, we need to be patient. Everyone knows John Newton's hymn, "Amazing Grace." But consider his early life. A foolish young man, he threw away opportunities. His drunkenness and bad behavior lost him posts on several ships. As he joked and drank, he was so obnoxious that one ship left him with a West African slave dealer, to whom Newton became enslaved for more than a year.

Were Newton's parents to blame? No, he rejected their teaching. We cannot judge their parenting by how Newton behaved. In any area, your child's failure or success does not determine your success or your worth. Like Newton's parents, we help, we pray, and we remember we don't see the whole picture yet, and that we are not in charge.

Chapter 7
Bad feelings

Have you let jealousy, resentment, grief, or guilt spoil your homeschooling? Like perfectionism, they can eat at you without your being aware of what they are doing to you and to your family.

Since everyone loves to talk about their children's accomplishments, it is easy to become jealous. Even when people don't brag, if our children are lagging, we notice. We can resent that our children are working harder for less reward. One child may spend hours agonizing over a writing assignment that others waltz through. The piano student that practices the most faithfully does not always get the most applause. The child who gets a D may work harder than the one with an A.

For those of us with children with learning challenges, there are more temptations to compare ours to others'. Ruth's son could read four years above grade level; mine only read three years below. Jon's child could count to a hundred when he was four; mine couldn't count to 60 when he was eight. How I longed for my son to be spared some struggles and enjoy the successes other kids have.

Are you grieving over your child's difficulties? We ache when our children have trouble making friends, learning to read, or keeping up with a new challenge, like high school courses. Several friends of mine have spent years trying to get a correct diagnosis of their children's physical difficulties or learning disabilities. A new diagnosis can make us grieve all over again. A new stage of life can bring us face-to-face with more effects of the disability or illness. We may have good reasons to grieve.

Sometimes we feel guilty. Are my child's struggles my fault? Why didn't I have the house tested for lead? Did I let them watch too much television when they were small? Was it something I did during pregnancy? Why didn't I realize sooner that my child needed a specialist?

We can be disappointed when our children don't do as well as others, without letting jealousy and resentment slip in. Grief is natural, but we need to watch ourselves that we don't let it fester. Guilt can overwhelm parents, if we let it. Even if we have reasonable regrets, we must not let them paralyze us. Fix what you can, and move on.

If you believe God is in charge and is wise and loving, then it follows that he must have a good purpose in allowing these difficulties, even if it is a purpose beyond our imagining. Do we believe that "for those who love God all things work together for good"? (Romans 8:28.) Do we trust Him when He doesn't do what we wanted for our children?

"Really, I'm fine," we tell ourselves. Guilt, grief, resentment, and jealousy can hide beneath the surface. If we are discontented in our homeschooling, we should take some time to reflect and pray for wisdom. Bitterness can slip into our hearts like a weed, and take over before we notice. We need to guard our hearts.

Some days I grieve over my son's learning difficulties. We think we hide our anxieties from our kids, but we don't. I remember one day, eighteen months into algebra, when I let those worries erupt. He had known how frustrating it was for me to have him struggling in something so easy for me. But that day I fumed aloud. When I finished, my teenager excused himself for a moment and returned with a typed sign, which he hung over our table:

Tis the way tis.

He was the teacher that day. We went back to work.

Whether it is jealousy, resentment, grief, or guilt, these attitudes have three things in common:

1. They don't help you.
2. They don't help your child.
3. They don't help you help your child.

If a child has a problem, struggle, or disability, God has allowed it and can use it for His glory. We need to pray and immerse ourselves in the wisdom of the Scriptures to help us see this is true.

But whether we are Christian or not, while we look for solutions, we can choose to accept what we cannot change. We must nurture and enjoy what we have. Emily Perl Kingsley's essay, "Welcome to Holland" is popular among parents of children with special needs, but relevant to all parents. As a metaphor for expecting a baby, she tells the story of a couple planning a trip to Italy, learning Italian, studying Italian guidebooks, eager to go. But when their plane unexpectedly takes them to Holland, they learn that if they give up their dreams of Rome and the Alps, they can enjoy the tulips and windmills, the art and the people. All parents have to adjust from what they expected to what they were given.

Chapter 8
How are we growing?

So far, we have discussed attitudes we need to weed out of our hearts and minds. But a good gardener doesn't just weed; she plants. As we weed out bad habits of mind, what are we planting? As we homeschool, we teach language arts, math, science, history, and the arts. We want our children to master the material, to learn to think and write. We can get so busy worrying about the academics of homeschool and the schedule that we forget we are more than a school. We need to focus on greater goals.

What are the goals of your homeschool? They vary with our beliefs. Christians want our children to love God wholeheartedly, though we often fail to live that way ourselves. But by God's great kindness, we have hope despite ourselves. Repentance, forgiveness, hope, and reliance on God's grace are the foundations of character.

But whether readers have those beliefs or not, all parents share other goals for our children. We want them to be useful, hard-working citizens. We want them to have friends and healthy relationships, to be honest, and to respect others. We all want them to be good neighbors. If their abilities permit, we want them to live independently and to be self-supporting. But if even if they cannot, they can make a difference by their kindness and care for others.

With goals like these, our homeschools are much more than schools. "Marriage is the true school of character," said Martin Luther. My husband adds, "Having children is the graduate school." We are not only the teachers; we are pupils. So as we consider character traits to build in our children, we also want to grow in these areas ourselves. Let me outline five:

Respect
Civilization depends on respect. When children are small, we teach them to respect others, not to bite them, or keep them awake at night. As our children grow, we want them to show respect in other ways. We teach our children to respect us as parents. When our children say, "Mom, there's nothing to do," sometimes I remind them I am not the cruise director, though I can provide chores or suggest ways to entertain themselves. I love to play with them, but I cannot do it all day. The universe is not revolving around them. My house should not, either.

Our children need to learn to obey, not slavishly, but as my pastor, David Coffin, says, "with cheerful alacrity." As Elisabeth Elliot wrote, we say no to them so that they can learn to say no to themselves and do hard things when they are adults. Our children need to learn to disagree respectfully, but trust our judgment. There will always be someone your child has to obey, no matter how old they are, so learning to get along with authority is a must.

If your child is not respecting you and resists your efforts to home-school, perhaps you need to read Betsy Hart, Dr. Kevin Leman, Ted Tripp, Paul Trip, or other experts on raising children. For a child with learning challenges, you also may you need to set up a structured system of rewards to help that child learn to connect actions with consequences. But it is possible you are doing the right things and just need to keep on consistently with your discipline.

We also need to respect our children. We must recognize that they are made in the image of God, and nurture their gifts, while we recognize their weaknesses. As they grow, our children change. Do not let past judgments write the future for your child.

Self-awareness

We want our children to know themselves, know their strengths, weaknesses, and tendencies. As they get older, asking questions is better than lecturing them. So often have we asked our son "What do you learn from this?" that it has become a family joke, but a valuable one. (His stock answer is, "Not to!")

Sometimes self-awareness comes naturally. Other children may need guidance. Paul Tripp's book, *Age of Opportunity*, offers wise advice in this area.

Praise good qualities when you see them in a child. One mother told me she never thought of her daughter as particularly patient. But the day a friend of hers told the daughter, "You are so patient," the girl began to think of herself as a patient person, and became more patient.

We all think in terms of stories. What sort of story do your children have about themselves? What does it tell them about themselves? Encourage them not to see their failures as an inescapable fate—"I'll never be good at this. I might as well give up"—but as weaknesses to learn from. We want them to reach the point of telling themselves, "I have to get to bed now or it will be hard not to be grumpy tomorrow." Encourage them to recognize what they are good at, what Robert Brooks calls "islands of competence."

Humility

Being humble does not mean hating yourself, but having a realistic view of yourself. Paul wrote a good definition in Romans 12: "Not to think of yourself more highly than you ought to think, but to think with sober judgment."

Being humble helps you get ahead. It makes it much easier to ask for help when you need it. In high school, my friend Meg was often the only person in math class willing to say, "I don't understand." Her humility helped many of us learn. Humility helps you be a better teammate. Not thinking too highly of yourself frees you to be happy about the accomplishments of others.

Being a humble homeschooler helps you help your children. We can admit we don't know, and then we can show how we get help. Otherwise my pride and ego can hurt my homeschool.

Perseverance

"Never, never, never, never give up!" said Winston Churchill. Much of his life can be seen as a series of failures, but because he knew how to keep going, he led Britain through its most difficult struggle in World War II. How do we help our children learn to keep going?

Some students do not learn perseverance for a long time, because schoolwork comes easily for them. High school math, for instance, was easy for me. But in my last year of college, it was a different story. I strained and struggled, and only passed my last math course with a C, and I was grateful it was not worse. That struggle helped me be a better teacher, because when I saw my son and other students struggling to pass, I remembered how it felt. All that work, the difficulty, the anxiety, and then finally, only a C! Not much to cheer about.

But when we teach a child at home and see them struggle, we can realize it is something to cheer about. When you see your children are not giving up, praise them. For some of our children, sitting down again to tackle work they find hard is heroic. If you do not praise your child for buckling down one more day to whatever they find hard, who will praise them? Those tough lessons—be it writing, spelling, memorizing, or whatever they struggle with—can build character.

My son astonished me one day by saying he was glad he was taking algebra because it taught him perseverance. He learned that word when he was nine, from a quotation that could have been our homeschool's motto: "By perseverance, the snail reached the ark," wrote Charles H. Spurgeon.

Remind children that life is more than schoolwork, and that the lessons are preparing them not just for college, but for life. Look for quotations and stories of perseverance to encourage your child.

Passion for learning

Children are born wanting to learn. If they have been discouraged by failures, revive the sense of wonder they were born with. Nurture their curiosity. Appreciate creation with them. Find what they like and care about, and built on that. Focus on their strengths.

Most of us need to be encouraged, as we grow older and busier, to stop and enjoy creation, whether it is smelling the lilacs, or stopping to look at the stars. We need to take our children outdoors. Let them observe, keep nature journals, and catch tadpoles. Charlotte Mason, the nineteenth-century British educator, saw how important this is. You will find good ideas in homeschool resources she inspired.

We also cultivate a love of learning by providing hands-on, out-of-the-house activities. Look for ways to take history out of the house, such as interviewing older relatives and neighbors, and visiting museums, historic sites, and re-enactments. Cultivate your local experts. Don't neglect art and music. Look for opportunities in your community.

What are your goals?

There is my list: self-awareness, respect, humility, perseverance, and passion for learning, built on a foundation of love for God and care for our neighbors. What is on your list? Take time to consider what you are aiming for, and it can help you decide what you can do without.

Part 2
Balancing our priorities

How do we keep our balance when there's so much to do? I have made many mistakes in parenting and homeschooling. I hope you can learn from them and from these basic principles that have helped me. We will look at taking care of ourselves in three areas:
- Our personal lives
- As teachers of our children
- Our marriages and families

Chapter 9
Take care of yourself

"Love your neighbor as yourself" implies that you should love yourself. Loving ourselves is not the most important part of life, but it equips us to care for others.

Loving yourself does not mean you don't make sacrifices. Parents work, sometimes in jobs they hate, to provide for their children. They sacrifice sleep to care for newborns. Especially in times of crisis, we sacrifice ourselves. The nearest many of us get to the sacrificial love Jesus demonstrated, laying down his life for his friends, is in our love for our children.

But the sacrifices we make do not cancel our duty to care for ourselves. Even if we face nothing traumatic, our large and small sacrifices can wear on us. We need to build time into our schedules to help ourselves keep going.

Time alone with God

We need to feed our souls. I think that begins with reading the Bible. If you disagree with me, try thoughtfully reading the Gospels daily for a month, and see if it doesn't challenge your spirit and stretch your mind.

Our goals for Bible reading need to be realistic. If you are a sleep-deprived parent of a new little one, this is probably not the stage of life for intensive study! Shorter readings are what we need to feed ourselves when our duties consume all our time. You may want to post favorite scriptures by the sink, or print a passage you want to memorize and keep it handy. Maybe you just have time to read one or two verses, and feel you scarcely have any brain cells left. God knows our situations. Pondering passages you already know can be a great help during those busy years, and are a wonderful habit anytime.

Another way we feed their souls is through worshiping God. Both public worship with others and private worship help orient us. In a storm, a compass can guide us even if we cannot see any landmarks. In the same way, though life may seem hard, dull, or crazy, when we spend time worshiping God, we are reminding ourselves of what is true.

We cannot see God, or heaven, or the immortal souls of those around us, but they are real. We need private time each day to read scripture, pray, meditate, and worship. Events you cannot control may make this short, you may be tired, but it is more important than brushing your teeth or drinking your morning coffee. Don't be discouraged when circumstances, laziness, or our distracted, reluctant hearts pull us from this time. Just keep turning back. Then through the day, we need to keep reminding ourselves of spiritual realities.

To keep our souls healthy, we also need to pray. Like Bible reading, this can be hard to manage if our children or small or disabled, or if we are short of sleep. God know what we can do, what we can't, and when we've chosen not to pray. We can pray through the day, making requests and giving thanks and praise as circumstances prompt us.

Having preschoolers helped me spiritually. Their ability to enjoy the beauty of a bright autumn leaf encouraged me to thank God for small beauties. Because of my children, now I am more likely to interrupt my work to look at a sunbeam filtering through the trees, and to admire a sunset or the stars, and to thank God. Thanking God with my children helped develop me that habit.

Not praying and not giving thanks shows I am acting as if God does not exist. Every Thanksgiving, people talk about "being thankful" or "feeling grateful." But here's a difference between a warm feeling that we have some good things, and taking time to thank the Maker for them. Remember the story of the ten lepers Jesus healed. Only one came back to say "Thank you."

Making time to pray as I should is a struggle, but we have to keep at it. If we think God is powerful, wise, generous, and loving, why wouldn't we pray? If we don't pray, how serious are our beliefs? That's what I must remind myself.

How to find the time? I discovered I liked getting up before the children and spending time reading the Bible and praying in a quiet

house. Others find it easier to find time later in the day. Meeting with
friends weekly to pray together also helped me keep going. Can't meet?
Try praying over the phone together.

There is nothing like having children to encourage us to ask for wisdom
(skill in godly living) for them and for us. As Julie Caprera said, "God will
give you exactly the children you need to drive you to your knees."

"Get Me to the Church on Time"

Getting to public worship isn't always easy, either. Circumstances will
conspire against it. So use all the tools you have to work toward it.
Make it a habit. Planning the day before helps: laying out clothes for
the children and yourself, having the breakfast things ready beforehand
and some easy lunch for afterwards. In our family, we find getting up
early helps. When our children were small, we realized we needed two
hours to get ourselves out the door Sunday mornings, much more time
than we needed other days. What helps us most is starting the night
before, by going to bed early. You get much more out of worship when
you are awake.

For parents of children with special needs, finding time to worship
can be a problem. At home these children need more care, so private
worship is hard. It is important to remember God knows what we have,
including how much time we have.

Several parents of children with special needs have told me that they
have not been able to bring their children to church. The change of
scene, the sounds, textures, and smells can be overwhelming for some
children with challenges. If our children are developmentally delayed,
we can feel awkward, bringing in a ten-year-old who acts like a six-year-
old. One couple told me they have not attended worship together in
years. Parents in this situation offered these suggestions for worship:

- Husband and wife can take turns attending services.
- When you visit a church, call ahead of time. Ask if there is a "cry
  room," a place where you and your child can hear the service but
  not be heard. If you briefly describe your child's needs, you may
  get help. (Don't be discouraged if they seem unprepared for your
  request; you might give them food for thought.)
- Don't be too quick to imagine everyone is judging you.
- If they are judging you, forgive them.
- If you are in a church and have established relationships, you can
  gently let your leadership know about your needs and the needs
  of other families with children with challenges.

That brings us back to all our families. As we raise our children to serve others, consider how you can help families with children with special needs. Carol Barnier shows one way, in the story of a highly autistic boy named Cory, who was very disruptive at church, making loud noises, not making eye contact, and unable to sit still in Sunday School. As Carol wrote:

> *Usually the child is simply thrust back into the hands of the already weary and overwhelmed parents with the added gift of "Sorry, but we just aren't prepared for this." But the head of this particular department.... got together a crew of teenagers.... They were taught about the extraordinary gift they would be giving to this child AND to his family by simply keeping Cory busy. So they took Cory to Sunday School. When he became disruptive, they took him for a walk. And they walked and they walked and they walked and they walked. Not only did it serve Cory and his family well, but it allowed these teenagers the vital privilege of really serving others in a concrete and highly appreciated way.*

[Source: sizzlebopblog.wordpress.com/2010/09/06/mean-adults-part-one/#more-161]

Stephanie Hubach has written two books to help you talk to your church about what might be done. Her new twenty-page book, *All Things Possible: Calling Your Church Leadership to Embrace Disability Ministry*, might make a good gift for yourself and your church. Her excellent first book, *Same Lake, Different Boat: Coming Alongside People Touched By Disability*, does the best job I have seen of explaining what I call the theology of disability: how the disabled fit into the body of Christ. They are not service projects; they are vital parts of the community.

Life to the fullest
Times with God—whether reading scripture and praying alone or in fellowship with others—strengthen us for the work he gives us to do. It helps us get our heads on straight for whatever comes and it gives us joy. Circumstances may be unhappy, dreary, even tragic. But for those who know God, who are looking forward to the place where tears will be wiped away, where these middle-aged, creaky bodies will be made new, and where we will see God face to face, there is hope. Heaven looks better every year. Make time daily to set your focus on God.

Chapter 10
Homeschooling: a lifestyle, not a life sentence

Feeling weighed down by your responsibilities teaching your children? Is homeschooling starting to consume all your waking thoughts? Perhaps you are taking this important work too seriously.

Don't homeschool 24/7. Don't let your children or their education become the center of your life. Raising my children may be the most important work I ever do, but making my children the focus of my life is not good for me—or for the children. Though the biblical language for this is idolatry (that is, making something other than God the center of my life), you don't have to believe in God to see that it isn't healthy. It's common sense that if you center your life around someone or something—even your children or their education—your life can get out of balance, one-sided, boring.

Are you aiming above all to raise children who are a credit to you? That is a kind of selfishness. We can tell ourselves we are working for our children's sake, when we are really aiming to enhance our reputation. A good test is how we react when things don't go as we wish. The next time your child falls short publicly, think about your attitude. Are you taking it too personally? In his article, "Solving the Crisis in Homeschooling," Reb Bradley discusses how we may be more concerned that our dreams for our children are fulfilled than we are with the children themselves.

Down in our hearts, we can become like toddlers, throwing a fit because we aren't getting what we want. But our children are not clay for us to mold as we wish, or make in our image. We can shape them, but they are their own persons with distinctive personalities and talents. We don't own them or their future.

Practically, how do we keep ourselves from spending all our waking hours working on or thinking about our homeschooling? Different kinds of people need different kinds of breaks:

- Talking to friends can refresh us.
- Fresh air and short walks can revive us. One homeschooler said when her four kids were old enough to be left alone briefly, it was a treat for her to walk down the street and look at the sky.
- Exercise helps us get in shape and sleep better. It can give us a mental break, when we focus on our form, not our homeschool.

- Creating an oasis our day can rejuvenate our minds. Maybe you need to take a few minutes in the afternoons to make a cup of tea, put your feet up, and read.

But some of you may be wondering how to get a break. Hire a sitter if your oldest is not old enough to keep an eye on the younger kids. Or swap babysitting with a friend weekly so you each get a free break. Perhaps a relative or friend with grown children can come regularly to give you an hour or two off.

If your children's special needs make it hard for you to get a babysitter, try to arrange events that give you a chance for adult conversation. Plan a regular trip to the playground or a play date, whatever allows your children to be fairly independent so you can have more adult interaction.

Even a short daily break at home can help. In our homeschool, we had daily "recess." My son played with his Legos® for thirty minutes downstairs, while I read upstairs. A mother with a teen with multiple disabilities will tell him when she needs to rest. He is allowed to use an educational PlayStation 2 game or computer program while she reads.

If you are a single parent homeschooling, or if your spouse is deployed or traveling extensively, it is especially important to take care of yourself by making breaks.

Six on, one off

Taking off one day a week is a new idea—and a very old one. Advertising, shopping, and buying are an important part of our culture, and encourage us to think more and more about acquiring stuff. Since the old "blue laws" that kept stores closed on Sundays have been repealed, we have lost that weekly break from commerce. Today, people feel deprived if stores are not open, even though technology makes it easy to spend money with a few clicks of a mouse or phone. Groups have started campaigns to take back some time from shopping: one day a year, one day a week, even a shopping-free Christmas season.

But the ancient Jewish practice was to take one day in seven, not to do your business, but as a day holy to God. That shows our need to get away from business is not a new need, driven by modern forces. Once we decide we will not work or shop, the whole pace of the day changes. What will we do? There is time for worship, rest, recreation, and family. There is time to reflect on the week just ending and on the week ahead. One mother I interviewed said her family found it very helpful to keep a weekly Sabbath. They worshiped and then went swimming or hiking together. My family also has found that having one day with time for worship, meals with friends, reading, talking, walks, and naps, has rested us for the week to come.

Though it takes planning for me to be sure that we will actually be able to rest on Sunday, it is worth the effort. On Saturday, I plan meals and check that we have all the groceries needed to get through Monday breakfast. Then we take Sunday off from chores. Unless it cannot wait, we don't do housework on Sundays.

When I was in college, I started taking Sundays off at the suggestion of my pastor. I have always found it refreshing, though not always easy to stick to. This day away from work has another benefit. Sometimes the break has given my husband and me new ideas for our work. Minds and bodies both benefit from rest.

Other pursuits

As we homeschool, we need to keep up other interests, as our circumstances permit. Our children will not thank us if they have become our obsessions. Find some other projects or hobbies. Remember, grading papers is not a hobby. Find something creative and enjoyable.

For those with small children, you may have little time, so start small. When my children were young, I enjoyed cross-stitching, but I had no time for it. So I took tiny projects when I went on vacation. Then, when the children were in bed, I could create a little hostess gift for my relatives while we sat talking. Sometimes small hobbies grow into second careers later. I did a little writing while my children were young, and when the youngest graduated, I started writing my first book.

If you aren't tending babies or others who need constant attention, there are more opportunities. Helping the family business or starting a small business of your own can help you be a better teacher by reminding you of the working world you are equipping your children for. Visiting the elderly, helping at a food pantry or homeless shelter, or any way of serving your community sets a great example for your children and will broaden your mind.

If your circumstances do not permit you to take time for hobbies or service outside the home, be patient. Maybe all you can manage is reading a few pages of a magazine occasionally. Life has its seasons. This season may feel like what my husband calls "life in the slow lane," but it will go by fast.

Longer getaways

Occasional overnight breaks can give you perspective, restore your patience, and let you sleep. Can a relative keep your children overnight so you and your spouse can get away? When a couple with six children took their first weekend alone together since becoming parents, you could tell afterward by the look on their faces how well the trip had refreshed them. The wife loves homeschooling their children, and is a conscientious, well-organized mother, but when she got back, she was glowing. "I had no idea!" she said, "We have to do this again."

More commonly, one parent will get away at a time. Perhaps Mom will take off for a homeschool conference to get perspective, insight, and a break. Being with other homeschoolers and hearing wise and humorous speakers can help you keep going, and it's also fun to shop when you can handle the merchandise, and maybe find little gifts or games for your children. Some moms go away for a weekend with friends. One mother of two teens, one with Aspergers, said she and her husband have "sanity weekends," where one of them gets away overnight. She checks into a hotel up the road, where she can read and relax, without laundry and lesson plans to nag at her. On her husband's sanity weekends, he prefers camping, enjoying the solitude of the woods.

If money or your child's special needs make it impossible to get away, you can still get an encouraging break by attending an online conference. Listening live to speakers over your computer or phone, chatting online with other homeschoolers who are listening to the same speaker, or even getting recordings to listen to later can encourage you. When I spoke at the *Ultimate Special Needs Expo* in the fall of 2011, one listener commented that she immediately took one of my suggestions on encouraging a child. Going into the next room, where her son was taking a math test, she tried the new idea and was rewarded with a huge smile. You too may find instant help through online conferences.

Know when you need an emergency break. One mother of a very hyperactive girl told me she occasionally sends her daughter off to her room to play quietly, saying "Mom needs a break now." As an Iowa mother told me, "Sometimes Mom is the one who needs the time out."

Chapter 11
Take care of your body

Want to live long enough to see your children grow up? Want to enjoy your later years more? Take care of yourself now.

What motivates you to get moving? For me, it was reading that between age forty and fifty, the average person loses ten pounds of muscle and gains fifteen pounds of fat. Since body fat burns fewer calories than muscle, I could imagine myself growing flabbier and more sluggish.

But if we are homeschooling, how do we find the time? Some parents told me they:

- take an exercise class,
- rollerblade as their children bicycle,
- plan a physical education activity three times a week to do with their children,
- jog on a treadmill in the mornings before the children are up,
- join a softball team,
- watch a movie as they use an exercise bicycle,
- play Dance, Dance, Revolution or Wii Sports,
- take walks with their spouse.

Hate exercise? As a child, I was so clumsy that team captains fought not to have me, so I understand why some of you may not want to exercise. It took decades to find exercise that I enjoyed. Let me encourage you to keep looking and keep trying. Start small. Find a friend to exercise with. Once I found an exercise class with encouraging teachers, it gave me a wonderful break from homeschooling. For those sixty minutes, I could not think about homeschool, because I was too busy trying to improve.

Even standing rather than sitting is good for you. As an experiment, I am writing this book standing at my desk. Almost immediately, I noticed that my back doesn't get stiff, that it is easier to make myself stop and do other tasks when I need to, and that I am less inclined to waste time surfing the Internet.

Getting outdoors and breathing fresh air is good for you. Some mothers have health problems that limit their activity. Even if you do not exercise, sitting outdoors or going for a drive is good for you.

Another key to good health is limiting your time on the computer. Computers, smart phones, and other gadgets open doors for us. We can get information, find online support groups, and locate tools to help our children. But computers can eat our time. Skimming, clicking, and jumping from page to page gives us the feeling of learning even when we aren't. And who hasn't succumbed to wasting time on stuff that is just plain silly? In *The Shallows: What the Internet Is Doing to Our Brains*, Nicholas Carr explains that increasingly the Internet is built to get us to skim and click, rather than to reflect and consider. He even cites evidence that using the Internet can increase distractibility. All those links that send us flitting around can keep us from remembering what we read as well as if we had read it in a book. The Internet affects not only what but how we feed our minds.

Feeding our bodies well also helps us keep going. I am no nutritionist, but it is obvious that drinking water or seltzer water is better than soda. Keeping a water bottle with me all the time helps me remember to keep sipping. When I complimented a friend on her weight loss, she told me she and her boys eat better since she starting keeping cubes of watermelon and peeled carrots in her refrigerator. Consider what snacks are convenient in your home. Are they the healthy ones? Know your weaknesses. Make yourself savor each bite of your treats. Don't inhale your chocolate. A friend of mine says the first and last bites of ice cream are the best, so he figures he does not need so many bites in between.

And while I am sounding like your mother, remember to get an annual check up with your physician. Afraid of bad news? Hiding from it will heal nothing. Some things are much easier to recover from when caught early. Take care of yourself so you can take care of your family.

What if you are worried about your mental health? Depression and other mental illnesses can slow us down and make it hard to get the help we need. Christians may even feel that depression, deep anxiety, and other difficulties are sins, but they are not. If you wonder if you are suffering from depression or other mental illness, seek help immediately.

Health is not just a subject we need to teach. We have to model how to take care of ourselves. When you go jogging, get that physical exam, eat healthy food, and take care of your body and mind, you are giving your children a good example. Take care of yourself so that you can nurture your children well.

Chapter 12
In the teachers' lounge

If I want people to think I am brave, I tell them I taught middle school. Teaching eighth graders math was fascinating. Sometimes they seem quite adult, then suddenly they act like goofy kids. You never know which way they will be. Two things helped me teach those 150 adult-children: having the time to think and plan, and the support of other teachers. The same two things helped me homeschool and should be helping you. If you are feeling stressed as you homeschool, ask yourself if you are taking advantage of these two great helps.

Time to think and plan
Whether you are an unschooler making phone calls to see where your child can take flying lessons, or a by-the-book homeschooler who prefers a very structured schedule, you are planning. Try to build regular planning time into your schedule, such as once a week or once a month.

I found it helpful to take time every couple of months to write myself a page or two on what we had been doing in our homeschool. I looked through my son's work and pulled a few pages to add to his portfolio. That writing helped me step back and see the big picture. Parts of it were discouraging—for example, I would be reminded how behind he was in math—but overall, it was delightful. Writing down the field trips we had taken and looking over my son's creative writing encouraged me. Even in the least productive, craziest times, taking the time to reflect always encouraged me that homeschooling was giving my son an interesting, customized education.

If you don't like to write, you could:
- Summarize the quarter (briefly!) to your spouse or to a friend, or record yourself a voice memo, or
- Keep a log of work finished on a spreadsheet as you go along and read it over occasionally. (My sister-in-law had her older children enter their work on the spreadsheet, so she did not even have to type it, just check it.)

Think you don't have time to ponder? Not taking time to think things over will cost you more time later. Like checking the directions on a new recipe or a long trip, it can save you lots of backtracking. Set aside a little time regularly to reflect on how your homeschool is going.

If you are writing out your children's weekly assignments, make yourself think of the big picture. If you aren't that organized, take time every quarter to see where you are. What goals did you set and how are you doing meeting them? Are you dreading to look at those goals because you are so far from them? Remember your goals guide you, not enslave you. If they are unrealistic, change them. It is your school.

Build time into your yearly schedule for goal setting and planning. A Maryland mom does this while her children are at summer camp. Every year after we visited the grandparents in Colorado, I spent the flight back considering how the year had gone, and wrote out goals, while my husband sat with the child who needed the most attention. Before you come home from a homeschool conference is another great time to stop and consider how your homeschool is going, and where it might go next. When a conference is over, I like to read my notes and make a one page list of what I want to do with what I learned, including books to read, websites to visit, and key ideas to ponder.

Taking time to read this book gives you an opportunity to make notes and think about what you can do to make next year more satisfying and less crazy.

Support

As a middle school teacher, even on the best days I looked forward to lunch in the teacher's lounge. Contact with the other adults reminded me I was not one, lone, sane adult shepherding my students through math. I was part of a team, on a mission to help educate these kids. Even when we didn't talk much, a smile or a nod in the hall reminded us we had companions in our mission.

Someone said the problem with homeschooling is that there is no teacher's lounge. I say, make one. Build support for your teaching. Here are some places to look for it:

1. Family

Your extended family can support your homeschool. Even if they are originally opposed to homeschooling, they may help. See what they enjoy sharing that might benefit your child: cooking lessons, oral history, teaching a skill, taking one or more children on a field trip—there are many ways to involve relatives. One Pennsylvania grandmother, a former opera singer, gave her granddaughters voice lessons weekly. Two homeschoolers with children with serious disabilities told me their children's friendships with their cousins gave them time to practice social skills.

My parents were very concerned when we started homeschooling. Though I had taught junior high math, could I teach a fourth grader to read? Would my son and I drive each other crazy? My father offered to come over once a week to be my substitute teacher, so I could get a break. I wrote plans and left a stack of work. But before long, my father was interested in doing more. With his love of history, he soon agreed to teach history one afternoon a week. The first few years I found curriculum and gave it to him. Then he began to write his own lesson plans, plan field trips, write and evaluate tests, and finally to help me choose textbooks. His take on this now: "I wish I had been able to do this with all my grandchildren."

2. Community

Your community can support your homeschool, too. Your neighbors and those you worship with can be surrogate grandparents, helping in all the ways listed above for families. If you ask, your local community center or recreation center may be willing to offer daytime classes for homeschoolers in swimming and other skills. They get more students; you get a physical education class and a little break.

Parks and historic sites are sometimes able to arrange daytime activities to support your homeschool group. As you get to know staff there, new opportunities may emerge. One mother told me how, after visiting a historic farm park, her son was able to get a job assisting there. My son worked one day a month as an apprentice re-enactor at a colonial farm, answering visitors questions, processing flax, and learning about life in the eighteenth century and about human nature as seen in tourists. Librarians save homeschoolers hundreds of dollars each year, and are eager to help you order books via Inter-Library Loan (ILL). Librarians also will help your child learn to research, and the facilities can provide your group meeting space.

Other public services and local businesses can support your homeschool, too. They may provide you with educational tours. As homeschoolers, we have been welcomed by bookbinders, police stations, courthouses, cola bottling plants, fire departments, and naval research facilities, to name a few. Local business owners and public servants can speak to your children as experts. Some may even mentor your older children in future careers.

3. Friends

One of the best parts of the teacher lounge was being able to commiserate. Make sure you have friends you can talk with, even if they are on the opposite coast. It will not help to spend all your time complaining about your children, but sometimes knowing that other people struggle with their children can help you keep going. They don't even have to be homeschoolers. One homeschooler with a daughter with attention deficit disorder told me that when times are tough, she calls a dear friend, who does not homeschool or have a child with AD/HD. But when the friend hears what has been happening, she has often replied, "That's just what my kid did!" Unless you spend lots of time with lots of children, you may not have a sense of what normal is for any particular age.

Sometimes finding friends can take time. Don't be discouraged. Keep trying.

4. Local support groups

Support groups differ in their structure. Some are just for parents, some offer weekly activities or outings, and others offer classes for your children. Some share one faith, some support one teaching style (such as classical or Charlotte Mason), others are based on other connections.

Groups also differ because of the personalities involved. You may need to try a few to find one that fits you. Keep an eye out for folks who understand your struggles. When I started homeschooling, helping my son learn to read and calculate was so hard that I thought I would scream if one more person said, "What I love about homeschooling is that we're always done by noon." Then I began to suspect that things were different at my friend Melody's house, so cautiously I asked. She laughed wryly, "We're lucky to be done by five!" I could have hugged her!

Keep an open mind as you look for support. Someone very different from you in situation and teaching style can still be a huge help, and you may help them.

If the support groups and co-ops you have tried have not worked out well for your family, try other groups. If that doesn't work, give it time. Groups change, people grow, move in, and move away, so don't burn bridges. Wait and see.

5. Online support groups

Online support groups have many advantages. You are more likely to find parents with a child like yours, using the same curriculum you use, or sharing your teaching philosophy. This is especially valuable if you have a child who is gifted, has learning challenges, or other disabilities—there are whole online groups devoted to homeschooling children with different challenges. You will find more variety online than in your local groups. You don't need to find time for a meeting, or get a sitter.

You post a comment or request to a list and get a reply whenever someone has time to write back. You can read it whenever you want.

But there are disadvantages. You can spend far too long at the computer, chatting about nothing, when you need to sleep or get work done. Exchanging posts or email messages with someone creates a false sense of intimacy. You may never know if your Internet friends have personal habits you find annoying, vile, or immoral. Sometimes people on the Internet are not what they seem. There are con artists and criminals around, so do not share last names, phone numbers, or other identifying information. And even the best intentioned friend on the Internet will never bring chicken soup over when your family is sick or give you a smile when you need one.

So I would recommend both. Join local groups, but if you have trouble finding support for your particular situation, look into online groups. After you join a group and introduce yourself, you may want to "lurk" for a while, that is, to read other people's posts without commenting or posting. That will give you the flavor of the group's conversations and character.

Special advice for special needs

If you are homeschooling a child with special needs, or if you have special needs yourself, here are some tips.

- Look for understanding, but don't insist on it. Insisting never helps.
- Look for ways to educate others gently about your family's needs. Don't get on a soapbox.
- Look for folks with similar special needs, either online or on the telephone.
- You may find special needs support groups understand your children and situation better than homeschoolers do, said a few parents I interviewed.
- A special education consultant can help you by telephone. Home School Legal Defense has special needs experts on staff. For longer-term help, you can hire a private special education consultant: several specialize in helping homeschoolers. Contact HSLDA or me for suggestions.
- Two groups deserve special mention: Joni and Friends, a Christian ministry reaching out to those affected by disability of all ages (not a homeschool organization), and NATHHAN, the National Challenged Homeschoolers Associated Network.

Help is out there—you just have to look for it.

Chapter 13
Healthy marriage and family

Home is more than a school. Homeschool is more than a way of life. Homeschools are part of families that grow out of marriages. A healthy marriage and healthy family relationships help us homeschool more happily and more effectively.

Healthy marriage

In most homeschools, the mother is the main teacher, but I have interviewed homeschooling fathers who do most of the teaching, so this is addressed to husbands and wives.

If you are married, you need to make time to be alone with your spouse. You need dates. Dates do not have to cost money: you just need time apart from the kids. You can take walks together or attend free concerts. My husband and I used to take "hardware store dates." We figured if we did not talk about the children more than half the time and if we got ice cream on the way home, it was a date. Two of my friends had a great Friday routine. She finished homeschooling at noon, then she and the boys cleaned the house. After work, her husband cooked his excellent spaghetti, which the boys ate early. The parents enjoyed a late dinner alone together.

Little things help. An older, wiser wife taught me to welcome my husband home with greeting and a kiss, and to straighten myself up a bit ahead of time. Unless it is an emergency, I try not to dump bad news or my frustrations on him as soon as he walks in the door. Give your spouse time to decompress from work and the commute. My husband prefers to eat supper before he is asked to advise and judge. Sometimes I am slow to figure out what the problems are, but now I know it is a bad idea to bring them up at bedtime! A wise pastor advised us that after the kids are in bed, even if we are not doing anything together, to try to be in the same room, not at opposite ends of our home. Look for little ways to nurture the relationship.

Whoever is teaching most, you need to involve your spouse in your homeschool. But ask yourself, "Am I giving too much information?" My tired husband's eyes will glaze over if I talk too much. It's not (usually) a lack of interest, and it has been good for me. Knowing he has limited time and energy forces me to stop and think over what he needs to hear. Summarizing for him helped me see the main points. Often the less-involved spouse can give perspective on homeschooling that we, bogged down in details, need.

But there is little point in asking for perspective if you are immediately going to disagree or dismiss it. Show your spouse respect. You may want to talk over how that communication is going. If you are brave and ready to hear the answer without feeling hurt, ask if your spouse wants to hear more or less about homeschool. What would he or she like to know?

If your spouse is uninvolved, Todd Wilson has suggestions. In an article in *The Virginia Home Educator*, he offers great advice to mothers on how to get fathers involved in the homeschool. His secret? "Whenever your husband involves himself in any way—LET HIM. You see, most of the time when a husband tries to help out, he gets told that he did it wrong. ... He makes a mental note never to do that again. And he doesn't." Wilson says that simple appreciation will be effective, while criticism, correction, and appeals for help will not.

But the main goal of conversation with your spouse is not how to improve your homeschool. The goal is to be happily married when the children are grown and gone. So talk about other stuff. When our children were young, a respected older man at church candidly told my husband that he had neglected this and that he was now working to find things to talk with his wife about. When you are empty nesters, you want to still be lovebirds and still be friends.

Homeschooling on your own

If you are a single parent homeschooling, or if your spouse is deployed or traveling extensively, both local and online support groups can help. There are resources for single parents homeschooling; check with your state homeschool organization or the Home School Legal Defense Association. More and more homeschool conferences are offering workshops for single parents, where you can make friends with other single parent homeschoolers who you can keep up with by phone or email for mutual encouragement. Many in the military community like homeschooling because of the flexible schedule and ability to customize curriculum to their children's needs and talents. Many bases have support groups that can help you.

Healthy family

Little kindnesses and acts can strength a marriage, and they can strengthen our families, too. Surprise your children with occasional small treats or fun activities. Leave your children little love notes. They encourage affection as well as writing, and you may receive some precious souvenirs in return.

Occasionally spend time alone with each your children. I have known fathers who, each Saturday, took one child out for a donut or other small treat. Be flexible, but let each one know he or she is special. In *Enjoy Your Middle Schooler*, former youth pastor Wayne Rice recommends simple outings with your child. They give you both time to practice listening and conversing. They help you and your teen prepare for the day they are grown adults. Listening becomes more important as children grow. Sometimes, sitting with my grown daughter an extra five minutes at a coffee shop, when I thought we had said all there was to say, has led us to more important topics. For more on conversing, I highly recommend Paul Tripp's book, *Age of Opportunity: A Biblical Guide to Parenting Teens*.

If you have children who need extra help, it is important to get time alone with your other children. But beware of what Carol Barnier calls "The Myth of Equal Time." In her excellent article by that name, she explains how she realized that it is not only an unrealistic goal, but an undesirable one, too. Consider that if God has given your family a child with special needs, then he knew what he was doing. So, she writes, look for the good this difficulty is bringing your other children. For example, my daughter has more compassion for those who struggle because of her brother. Each child does not need to have an equal share of your waking hours. As Melinda Boring, mother of two with attention deficit disorder and author of *Heads Up Helping*, wrote, "Children, being fair means giving you what you need when you need it."

Finally, laugh together. "A cheerful heart is good medicine," says Proverbs 17:22. So be ready to laugh at a joke, an odd situation, even your own mistakes—and your child's, too, if he or she will join you. Enjoy word play and puns. Most children around age seven start enjoying corny jokes, so get them joke books at the library. Even your child who hates reading will read it to himself. (And unfortunately to you, too, but try to smile.) Does your family prefer slapstick? Watch old Charlie Chaplin or Laurel and Hardy movies together, or other comedians you enjoy. Laughter is important. It cannot be scheduled, so watch for it and savor it.

Above all, enjoy your time with your children. When you homeschool, you have rare opportunities to custom tailor their education. Even better, you have more time to develop character and relationships. Build on a foundation of love and enjoy the gift of having children.

Sources and Resources

Barnier, Carol. *The Big WHAT NOW Book of Learning Styles.* Lynnwood, Washington: Emerald, 2009.

_____. *If I'm Diapering a Watermelon, then Where'd I Leave the Baby? Help for the Highly Distractible Mom.* Lynnwood, Washington: Emerald, 2004.

_____. "The Myth of Equal Time." http://www.crosswalk.com/family/homeschool/encouragement/the-myth-of-equal-time-11552735.html August 29, 2007. Accessed October 11, 2011.

Baskin, Amy and Heather Fawcett. *More Than a Mom: Living a Full and Balanced Life When Your Child Has Special Needs.* Bethesda, Maryland: Woodbine House, 2006.

Boring, Melinda L. *Heads Up Helping: Teaching Tips and Techniques for Working with ADD, ADHD, and Other Children with Challenges.* Victoria, British Columbia: Tafford, 2002.

Bradley, Reb. "Solving the Crisis in Homeschooling: Exposing the 7 major blind spots of homeschoolers." http://www.familyministries. com/ under "Free," subheading is "Family Life." Accessed October 11, 2011.

Brooks, Robert, Ph.D. *The Self-Esteem Teacher.* Loveland, Ohio: Treehaus, 1991.

Carr, Nicholas. *The Shallows: What the Internet Is Doing to Our Brains.* New York: Norton, 2011.

Elliot, Elisabeth. *The Shaping of a Christian Family: How My Parents Nurtured My Faith.* Grand Rapids, Michigan: Revell, 2005.

Harris, Greg, interviewed by Jennifer Olmstead in "Outgrowing the Greenhouse," The Home School Court Report, Vol. XXV, No. 3— Cover Story. hslda.org/courtreport/V25N3/V25N301.asp Accessed October 11, 2011.

Hart, Betsy. *It Takes a Parent*. New York: Putnam, 2005.

Hubach, Stephanie. *All Things Possible: Calling Your Church Leadership to Embrace Disability Ministry*. Agoura Hills, California: Joni and Friends, 2010.

_____. *Same Lake, Different Boat: Coming Alongside People Touched By Disability*. Phillipsburg, New Jersey: P&R Publishing, 2006.

Ingersoll, Barbara, and Sam Goldstein. *Lonely, Sad, and Angry: How to Help Your Unhappy Child*. Plantation, Florida: Specialty Press, 2001.

Pashler, Howard, et.al. "Learning Styles: Concepts and Evidence." *Psychological Sciences in the Public Interest*. Vol. 9. No. 3. December 2008, pp. 105-119.

Rice, Wayne. *Enjoy Your Middle Schooler*. Grand Rapids: Zondervan, 1994.

Steere, Cathy. "Kick Off Your Running Shoes!" http://www.heav.org/resources/articles/struggling-learners/kick-off-your-running-shoes.html Accessed October 11, 2011.

"Theory of Multiple Intelligences." http://en.wikipedia.org/wiki/Theory_of_multiple_intelligences#Intrapersonal Accessed October 14, 2011.

Tripp, Paul. *Age of Opportunity: A Biblical Guide to Parenting Teens*. Phillipsburg, New Jersey: P&R Publishing, 1997.

Welch, Edward T. *Running Scared: Fear, Worry, and the God of Rest*. Greensboro, North Carolina: New Growth, 2007.

Wilson, Todd. "Getting Your Husband Involved in Homeschooling," *Virginia Home Educator*. Richmond: Home Educators Association of Virginia, Winter 2008.

Wolfe, Paul D. *Setting Our Sights on Heaven: Why It's Hard And Why It's Worth It*. Carlisle, Pennsylvania: Banner of Truth, 2011.

CPSIA information can be obtained
at www.ICGtesting.com
Printed in the USA
LVHW082134051020
667984LV00021B/4440

9 780981 938912